101 HOLIDAY GIFT IDEAS

BARBOUR
PUBLISHING

101
HOLIDAY
GIFT IDEAS

Published by Barbour Publishing, Inc., P.O. Box 719, Uhrichsville, Ohio 44683, www.barbourbooks.com

Our mission is to publish and distribute inspirational products offering exceptional value and biblical encouragement to the masses.

 Member of the
Evangelical Christian
Publishers Association

Printed in the United States of America.
5 4 3 2 1

CONTENTS

Like the wise men, we give because the Lord first gave to us. The homemade touch puts an extra special quality on any gift. Going the homemade route can save money, and it doesn't have to take lots of time. The best gifts, though, aren't those with a high price tag or those at the top of the popularity list. They are the ones that come from the heart.

There are no great things,
only small things with great love.
Happy are those.
MOTHER TERESA

SIMPLY SPECIAL GIFTS

"Freely you have received, freely give."
MATTHEW 10:8

FAMILY COOKBOOK

Organize your recipe box and create a special gift in the process. Take all those old handwritten recipe cards, newspaper clippings, and flagged cookbooks, and type the recipes into your computer. Be sure to include a note with each recipe that states who made it stand out and how it became a family favorite. If you have a handwritten recipe from a special relative who is now deceased, you may want to photocopy or scan it to preserve the handwriting as a piece of history. You can even divide your recipes according to the cooks and include their pictures. Place the pages on durable paper and bind them in a ringed binder that can be added to as more recipes become family treasures.

FAMILY PHOTOS

It sounds too easy and even a bit egotistical, but distant (and not-so-distant) relatives and friends love to receive pictures of you and your growing family. You don't have to go to the expense of a professional portrait. A good snapshot with a pretty background will do fine. Buy an inexpensive frame for it. Or, collect several snapshots from special occasions throughout the year and put together a small photo album.

FAMILY HISTORY BOOK

Put your computer to work. Scan old family photos. Get as many pictures of grandparents and notable relatives as you can find—showing them young and old. Arrange the pictures on pages, starting with the oldest, and type an explanation of who the people were, when and where they lived, and any unique information you can provide about them. Use the photos and descriptions to trace family history and pass on important family notes about faith, traditions, and health. Print the pages on paper with some weight and durability. Use a three-hole punch and bind the pages in a small, ringed binder or have a print shop bind your booklet. Make multiple copies so each individual in the family has one.

Memory Books

These are perfect gifts for the hard-to-buy-for relative. Purchase a small blank journal or autograph book and write down some special, funny, and heartwarming memories about the person you will give it to. If time allows, pass the book around to other relatives and friends and have them contribute a short note. Embellish pages with stickers, drawings, small photos, and the like. It is sure to be a gift that will be cherished for years to come.

Simple Homemade Soap

Grater
Bar soap remains (mild soap like Ivory
  works well)
Water
Food coloring
Perfume or potpourri oil
A mold (specially bought plastic soap mold,
  cookie cutters, or even an ice-cube tray)

Grate soap pieces into a powdery texture. Mix with just enough water to create a thick paste.

Add a drop or two of food coloring and fragrance. Knead the mixture until it is thick like dough; press the mixture into a mold, or roll the soap into balls. Let it dry for at least 24 hours. For a simple gift, tie a ribbon around the homemade bars of soap or fill a small gift basket with little soap shapes.

BATH BOMBS

In a glass bowl, mix 1 part citric acid (you can get this at a pharmacy) with $2\frac{1}{4}$ parts baking soda. Add several drops of essential oil and a few drops of food coloring. Moisten by spraying with water or witch hazel (witch hazel works better because it evaporates more quickly) until mixture just begins to stick together. Shape truffle-sized balls (1-inch diameter) of the mixture. Let the bombs dry and harden for 24–48 hours. Pack each bomb into its own paper candy cup. Store bombs in a closed container. To use, drop 1–3 into warm bath water.

Scented Bath Salts

2 cups Epsom salts
1 cup sea salt, rock salt, or coarse salt
Food coloring (green or blue, optional)
¼ teaspoon glycerin
4 or 5 drops essential oil for fragrance
    (vanilla, citrus, or peppermint)

Combine salts in a large glass or metal mixing bowl and mix well. Add food coloring, a few drops at a time, until desired color is achieved. For white salts, simply skip the coloring. Add glycerin and essential oil and mix well. Spoon salts into clean, dry jars with cork stoppers or metal screw-on lids and seal. Makes 3 cups of bath salts. When giving as a gift, attach a label identifying the scent and recommend using ⅓ to ½ cup in the bath.

Sinus-Headache Pillows

Flax seeds
Eucalyptus leaves
Crushed spearmint leaves
Rosemary leaves
Crushed peppermint leaves

Whole lavender buds
⅛ yard cotton fabric
Ribbon

Blend the herbs. Cut two pieces of fabric 4x10 inches and sew right sides together with a ¼-inch seam. Leave a 2-inch opening. Turn it right side out and stuff with the herb mixture. Sew opening closed. Tie a ribbon around the middle with a tag including directions to use as a reliever of headaches.

HERB SACHETS

1 handful each of dried lavender flowers and
   rosemary
1 tablespoon of crushed cloves
Small pieces of dried lemon peel
Cotton fabric cut into 4x4-inch squares

Blend the herbs in a bowl. Place right sides of two fabric squares together and sew a ¼-inch seam, leaving a 1-inch opening. Turn the right sides out and stuff the square pouch with the herb mixture. Sew the opening closed. (Sew a loop of ribbon onto a few sachets so they can be hung over a clothes hanger.) Wrap several sachets together in tissue paper tied with raffia. Attach a note explaining that these should be placed in drawers, closets, and boxes to protect clothing from insects and to add freshness.

PINECONE FIRE STARTERS

Paraffin or old candle stubs
Scented oil (cinnamon, bayberry, or citrus spice)
Candlewick
Several dry pinecones

Melt the wax in a coffee can placed in a pan of water. Add a few drops of oil to melted wax. Wrap or tie a length of wick around the top of each pinecone. Dip pinecones into melted wax several times, allowing wax to harden between dips. For gift-giving: Present them in a small basket with a note of instruction to add 2–3 pinecones to fire kindling and light the wicks.

Mosaic Coaster

Acrylic paint
4-inch clay saucer
Small pieces of broken stained glass or
   colored tile
Heavy craft glue
Tile grout
1 thin sheet of cork

Paint the saucer—except for the bottom of the inside where the glass will be glued on. Allow paint to dry completely. Arrange pieces of glass on the bottom inside of the saucer, covering the entire area. When you have a pattern set, start gluing one piece at a time. Just a dab of glue will do. As the glue sets for about 30 minutes, prepare your grout. Spread the grout over all the glass and gently press it into the spaces between each piece. Let it set about 10 minutes; use a damp sponge to wipe extra grout from the surface of the glass and along the painted sides of the saucer. Allow the grout to dry overnight. The last step is to glue on a circle of cork that is just a bit smaller than the bottom of the saucer. As a finishing touch, you can apply a grout sealer to protect the white grout from stain.

Scented Coasters (and Trivets)

Prequilted material
Thread
Granulated potpourri from a paper sachet

Cut two 3–4-inch circles or squares from the prequilted material. Pin them together with right sides facing. Stitch them together, leaving a hole large enough to insert potpourri. Turn stitched pieces right side out and press with a warm iron. Fill with potpourri. (You may want to make larger ones as trivets.) When you place a hot container or cup of tea on the coaster or trivet, the heat will activate the aroma.

Lighted Potpourri Jar

1 string of 18–25 white Christmas lights
1-quart canning jar
Potpourri
4–6-inch lace or crocheted doily

Place the end of the light string that does not have the plug in the bottom of the jar. Add a handful of potpourri. Start winding the light string into the jar, stopping occasionally to add more potpourri. When the jar is full, let the cord with plug hang out and cover the top with the doily. Secure the doily in place by tying raffia or ribbon around the edge. When you plug this in, the low heat generated from the lights will warm the potpourri and fill the room with fragrance.

DECORATIVE CURTAIN

1 yardstick
Paint
1 skein of yarn
1 big bag of neon-colored drinking straws
1 bag of colorful beads

Take a yardstick (often given away by lumber companies) and drill a hole at every inch marker. Drill against a piece of scrap lumber to keep the yardstick from cracking. Paint the yardstick, then cut the yarn in 5–6-foot lengths, and tie one end of each length through a hole in the yardstick. Cut the straws in thirds (about 2 inches per section) and thread them onto the yarn. Add a bead (or even a fake flower) every so often. When you reach the bottom of the yarn, secure a large bead for weight. When done, the curtain should fit across the average doorway.

Exercise Mat

2 terrycloth beach towels (approximately
  28x49 inches)
1 sheet of thick foam from a fabric or
  upholstery store cut 2 inches smaller than
  the size of one towel
2 elastic strips 30 inches long and 2 inches
  wide

Pin the towels together and stitch a ¼-inch seam, leaving an opening of at least 6 inches. Trim the corners and turn right sides out. Insert the foam. Hand-stitch the opening closed. For each piece of elastic, sew the ends together to make a circle. Use these elastic circles to slip over the mat when it is rolled.

Heating Bag

This little bag is very nice for soothing little aches and pains or warming cold feet.

½ yard of flannel (cotton) fabric
18 inches of 1-inch-wide cotton webbing,
  cut into 2 equal pieces
4 cups uncooked rice
1 tablespoon whole cloves

Cut the flannel into a 14x18-inch rectangle. Fold, right sides facing, to 7x18 inches. Mark each short end at the fold with a straight pin; unfold. For handles: Pin one end of webbing 1 inch from the fold; pin remaining end 1¾ inches from the cut edge. Repeat for opposite handle on other short end. Fold fabric in half, right sides facing with handles sandwiched inside. Pin the edges allowing a ¾-inch seam, and sew the bag together, leaving a 3-inch opening along the long side. Clip the corners and turn the bag right side out. Fill with rice and cloves, then hand-sew the opening closed. To use as a heating pad, microwave for 1–2 minutes on high. Remove from microwave, using the handles.

KID'S DRESS-UP CHEST

Buy a large, plastic storage box with lid. Paint the sides with fabric or acrylic paints. Use the child's name in your design. Then go to yard sales and thrift shops, collecting several pieces of unique clothing—like a wedding dress and veil, prom dresses, ballerina's tutu, uniforms, costumes, and the like. Also look for extravagant hats, shoes, purses, and jewelry. Fill the storage box, and give the gift of hours of imaginative fun.

KID-INVOLVED GIFTS

It is good to be children sometimes,
and never better than at Christmas,
when its mighty Founder was a child Himself.
A CHRISTMAS CAROL, CHARLES DICKENS

"If you, then, though you are evil,
know how to give good gifts to your children,
how much more will your Father in heaven
give good gifts to those who ask him!"
MATTHEW 7:11

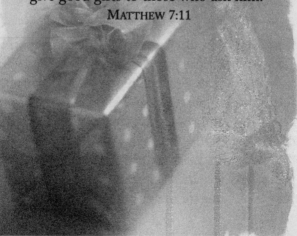

A Special Bookmark

This one's sure to please Grandma and Grandpa! Gather old and new pictures of your family and trim them to fit on a piece of heavy paper that is approximately 2x7 inches. Arrange photos on the front and back and secure in place with glue. You can add the date, a Scripture, or sentiment, etc. Have the bookmark laminated, or cover it with clear contact paper.

Photo Puzzle Cards

Get a large print made of a favorite family photo. Mount the photo to green or red poster board with spray adhesive or a light, even coating of glue. When dry, write a greeting on the back side. Help the child use scissors to cut the photo into 8–12 pieces. Place in an envelope and mail. (You may want to place the puzzle in a small plastic bag before placing it in the envelope.)

Puzzle Picture Frame

Pick up an old jigsaw puzzle or two from a garage sale (the more colorful the pieces, the better). Fashion a square, triangle, or hexagon out of craft sticks by gluing them together. Then glue the jigsaw pieces on the sticks. Make a wide frame with enough space in the middle to attach a picture to the back. Cut out lightweight cardboard in the same size and shape as the stick frame, and glue it behind the picture. Attach string or ribbon to hang this ornament to your tree or a magnet for refrigerator displays. (Hot glue makes the project quick but requires supervision when children are involved.)

Plaster Handprint

In a large disposable container, mix together 1 cup of water and 2¼ cups of plaster of paris until it is thick but pourable. Pour into an aluminum pie plate. When the plaster is firm enough to hold a shape, have the child press his or her hand into it and carefully lift up. Allow the child to press some marbles, seashells, or other small embellishments into the plaster, but leave the handprint untouched. Let the mold dry completely overnight. Record the date and the child's name on back.

FRAGRANT SOAP BALLS

Ivory Snow Flakes
Perfume or scented oil
Food coloring

Use water to moisten the soap flakes to a consistency likened to very stiff dough. Divide the mixture into several bowls. Add a different perfume and food coloring to each bowl for variety. Have children shape large spoonfuls of the soap into balls. Place the balls on trays (labeled with their molder's name!) to harden for several days. Have each child wrap his or her soap balls in colored cellophane paper and tie the package with a pretty ribbon.

QUILTED PILLOWS

For a good way to get children to learn simple

sewing skills, try this: Gather fabric scraps (preferably cotton) and cut 9 squares, approximately 4x4 inches. Help your child sew the pieces together by hand to form one 12x12-inch square (for younger children you might want to use only 4 squares that are 6x6 inches so there is less sewing to do). For the back side, you can do another set of 9 squares, or you can choose one piece of fabric that measures 12x12 inches. Place both 12-inch-square pieces with right sides facing and sew around the edges, leaving a small section open to flip it right side out. Fill with polyester stuffing and sew up the opening.

GINGERBREAD PEOPLE

Gingerbread-man cookie cutter
Pencil
Scissors
Medium-grade sandpaper
Cinnamon stick
Bowl
Measuring spoons
Powdered white tempera paint
White glue
Squeeze bottle

Yarn
Hole punch

Using a gingerbread-man cookie cutter as a pattern, trace and cut out shape on the back of the sandpaper. For gingerbread smell, rub the sandy side of sandpaper with the cinnamon stick. In a bowl, stir together 2 teaspoons of paint with 4 tablespoons of glue; spoon into squeeze bottle. Draw features and details of gingerbread man with squeeze bottle, let dry, and hang by a yarn threaded through a hole punched in top of gingerbread man.

Decorative Light Switch Cover

Gather 9 Popsicle sticks (the amount used can vary with size of light cover), craft glue, a sheet of craft foam, and foam craft shapes. Use the existing light cover to cut the foam sheet to fit the switch area. Mark the center opening with a pen and use a utility knife to cut an opening in the center of the foam. Place 1 stick against the switch and mark where to cut the opening. An adult should help with the sharp scissors or a utility knife to cut the stick. Glue the sticks onto the foam, straight and touching. The sticks should hang over the edges of the foam just a bit to cover it. Decorate the switch cover with paint and foam shapes. When the switch cover is completely dry, use double-sided tape to attach it to the existing switch plate cover.

GLASS AQUARIUM

Glass container
Sand or decorative gravel
Artificial greenery
Shells, stones, or marbles
Glass fish with floats

Select a fish bowl, a regular bowl, or a decorative bottle or jar for your aquarium. If you choose a glass container with a lid, it will require less cleaning and the water will not evaporate as quickly. Start with some sand or gravel on the bottom and anchor your greenery into it. Add some seashells or glass marbles for interest. Slowly pour water into the aquarium (you can color the water with food coloring), then add the floating glass fish.

Tub-Time Toys

Pencil
Paper
Scissors
Soft sponges (variety of colors)
Felt-tip marker with permanent ink

Create your own animal patterns (duck, fish, alligators) and cut out. Draw around each pattern on a dry sponge using the felt-tip marker. Soak the sponges in water and then squeeze them out as dry as you can. Cut inside the marker line with scissors, squeezing as you cut.

Decoupage Band-Aid Boxes and Candy Tins

Acrylic paints in colors of your choice
Tins
Small paintbrush
Flowers cut from cards, gift wrap, or wallpaper
Glue
Can of spray varnish
Wide band of lace (for bottom of candy tin)

Paint tins inside and out. Cut out flowers to fill surfaces and glue all over front, top, and sides. Coat with spray varnish. To create an elegant effect on candy tin, a wide band of lace may be glued around bottom portion instead of flowers.

SNOW GLOBE

Clean a glass jar that has a lid. (Small jam or peanut butter jars work well, but avoid the ones with the "fresh test button" on the lid.) Fill the jar with water, screw on the lid, and turn it upside down for a while to see if the seal will hold water. Paint the outside of the lid with a coat or two of acrylic paint. Arrange a grouping of clean plastic (or otherwise waterproof) items on the inside of the lid. Glue them in place with a water-resistant glue. When the glue has dried, fill the jar with water and add approximately 1 teaspoon of gold or silver glitter. Put a tiny ribbon of glue around the inside edge of the lid and immediately screw the lid tightly onto the jar.

GLOVE PUPPETS

Buy inexpensive ladies' knit gloves. For each glove, gather five 1-inch pom-poms and ten 5-millimeter wiggle eyes. You'll also need thick craft glue and 5 tongue depressors. Each pom-pom will be a head. First glue the eyes in place. A tiny pom-pom or sequin can be added for a nose. Ears made of felt can be glued to the back. Be creative with embellishments. Before putting the head onto the end of the glove finger, insert a tongue depressor inside the finger and allow the glue to set before removing the stick.

SPOON PUPPETS

Gather wooden spoons and embellishments like 7-millimeter wiggle eyes, foam shapes, fabric and ribbon remnants, paint, and markers, including hot or craft glue. Start by painting your spoon. The back of the spoon will be the face area. You may want flesh color above where the spoon narrows to the handle and a bright color along the handle. Set eyes in place with glue. Use a sharp permanent marker to add a smile. Cut small circles out of foam for cheeks, nose, and ears. Glue in place. Tie ribbon to the "neck." Use thin strips of fabric or ribbon for "hair." Be creative.

To make a snowman: Paint your spoon all white. Set eyes in place. Use a long teardrop-shaped orange foam piece for nose and small circles of foam in red or pink for cheeks. Paint a 2-inch straw hat black and add a holiday ribbon to the neck for a scarf.

TURTLE TRINKET BOX

2 clay saucers, 4 inches in diameter
4 clay pots, 1½ inches tall
Acrylic paint
Small foam ball
2 wiggle eyes

Paint the saucers and pots with acrylic paint (green is great for this project). You can add a shell design to one saucer that will be used on the top side of the turtle's shell. Paint some toes on the clay pots on the outside edges with the opening facing down. Paint the foam ball, adding face detail as you like. Allow the paint to dry. Use heavy craft glue to attach the foam ball to the saucer that will be the top, facedown. Place the bottom saucer facedown on your table, then glue the bottom of the pots to the bottom of the saucer. When dry, place the rims of the saucers together. The top lifts off when you are ready to place trinkets inside.

Decoupaged Bottles

Clean, clear glass or plastic bottles, jars,
   vases, or bowls
Colorful tissue paper
White glue
Paintbrush

Make sure whatever you are decoupaging is clean, dry, and dust-free. Rip or cut tissue paper into different shapes. Water down the glue just a bit. Brush glue on small areas of object you are decoupaging. Place colored tissue in desired pattern. Paint a little more glue on top of tissue. Let dry. It's best to work on a protected surface. Place gifts like a candle, bath salts, or homemade potpourri inside the finished bottles.

HOMEMADE DECORATIONS TO SHARE

"We will share with you whatever good things
the LORD gives us."
NUMBERS 10:32

Fabric Garland

Twine, jute, or heavy string
Scraps of cotton Christmas fabric and even
    some plain colors and muslin

Cut a length of twine at least 6 feet long. Tie a
loop in one end. Cut fabric in strips measuring
1x6 inches. Tie the fabric onto the twine—knot
in the middle and equal amount of fabric on both
sides. Alternate fabrics as you go. Keep the pieces
close together for a full effect to your garland.

You'll want at least 24 feet for an average 6-foot
tree. You can also drape this garland across your
curtain rods or around your banister.

Rag Tree

A straight twig 8–14 inches long and as
    thick as a kindergartner's pencil
A base out of a branch 1½ inches tall and
    2 inches in diameter
Glue
⅛ yard of cotton fabric in Christmas color
Pinking shears

24–36 tiny pinecones no more than ¼-inch tall

Whittle the smallest end of the twig to a point. Match a drill bit to the other end of the twig and drill a hole in the base piece at least 1 inch deep. Glue the twig into the hole. Cut strips of fabric with pinking shears, ¾-inch wide by 6 inches long. Tie the first strip just below the pointed tip of the twig. Add strips, keeping them close and altering the direction the ends hang. When the twig is full, use the pinking shears to trim the ends of the fabric to vary the lengths—longest at bottom to shortest at top. Glue a small pinecone to the end of each fabric strip.

SCENTED TREE ORNAMENTS

1 cup applesauce	Waxed paper
2 tablespoons nutmeg	Cookie cutters
¾ cup cinnamon	Drinking straws
2 tablespoons ginger	Fabric paint
2 tablespoons ground cloves	Sequins

Mix all ingredients together. Roll onto waxed paper to ⅛-inch thickness. Cut out with cookie cutters. Poke holes for hangers with a drinking straw. Put on a wire rack and allow to dry for 3 days, turning daily. Use fabric paints, sequins, and other embellishments to dress them up. Makes approximately 1 dozen ornaments.

CANDY-COATED ORNAMENTS

Buy several small foam balls. Spread a coating of glue over the ball and glue on your favorite candy. Red cinnamon candies, crushed peppermint sticks, round peppermints glued on their narrow sides, gumdrops, M&Ms, or any other fun candy will work (best to use just one variety of candy per ball). Use a long straight pin to secure a loop of ribbon to the top for a hanger.

JEWELED CHRISTMAS BALLS

Solid-colored round Christmas ornament
Juice glass
Tweezers
Round multicolored jewels (available in craft
stores)

Tacky glue
Gold glitter paint pen

Set ornament on juice glass to stabilize; using tweezers, dip jewels in tacky glue and arrange on upper half of ball; allow to dry. Using paint pen, circle each jewel and dry. Turn ornament over and repeat for bottom half.

GINGERBREAD-FRIENDS GARLAND

This garland will give your home a "country" feel.

Clay gingerbread men
⅛-inch-wide red ribbon
Red and white icing
Scissors

Using oven-bake clay, make a batch of gingerbread men. Punch holes in each hand with a drinking straw and bake. After the "cookies" have cooled, outline and decorate using icing. Link the men together by threading thin ribbon through holes in their hands. Knot ribbon and trim the ends. Drape over mantel or along edges of country cupboard.

COOKIE-CUTTER PHOTO ORNAMENTS

Trim a favorite photo to fit inside a cookie cutter shape. Glue the edges of the picture to the inside of the cutter. You can add ribbon, lace, glitter, and paint to the cutter as desired. Remember to label the picture with name and date. Hang on the tree. Make a collection of these ornaments to show the growth of a child or changes in the family's appearance over the years. (A great gift for Grandma!)

FABRIC-FUSED WOODEN ORNAMENTS

From a craft store, buy simple wooden shapes cut from $1/8$-inch plywood (stars, trees, bells, etc.). Sand the rough edges and wipe them clean. Lay an old towel or sheet over your ironing board. Spread a large piece of holiday fabric (cotton) on the ironing board facedown. Place a matching-sized sheet of fusible web on it with paper side up. Cover with a thin towel and use a hot iron to press the webbing on according to the directions. When cool, peel the paper away. Set your wooden shapes on the covered ironing board.

Keep them close together (about ½-inch apart). Lay the fabric over them with web side against the wood. Cover the fabric with a thin towel, and use the iron to fuse the fabric to the wood. Next, place the piece of fabric facedown on a cutting board, and use a utility knife to cut around the wood shapes. Touch loose fabric with a dot of glue. Add embellishments like tiny wooden stars or buttons. Paint a name on either the fabric or wooden side. The back side can be left plain, painted, or fused with fabric. Lastly, use a tiny bit to drill a hole in the top of the ornament. Hang by gold thread or floss.

ETCHED-GLASS ORNAMENTS

These lovely ornaments are easier to make than they look.

Clear round glass ornament
White vinegar
Paint pen (available in craft, discount, and
    fabric stores)
¼-inch-wide masking tape
Star stickers
Rubber gloves
Paintbrush

Etching cream (available in art, craft, and
   discount stores)
Key chain
Sprig of greenery

Before starting, clean glass ornament with hot
water and white vinegar. (Be sure not to reintro-
duce fingerprints to areas that will be etched.)
Use paint pen to draw snowflake designs and/or
masking tape to create stripes. Press star stickers
firmly to ornament. After paint has dried, put on
rubber gloves and etch ornament according to
instructions using brush and etching cream.
Wash off etching cream, and carefully remove
stickers, tape, and paint. A beautiful frosted or
etched surface will remain. Thread key chain
through ornament hanger and tuck sprig of
greenery into top of ornament.

ELEGANT CRÈCHE ORNAMENT

1 Styrofoam ball
Paint
Heavy craft glue
Short pins
2 sizes of small beads
Sequins

1 tiny plastic baby
2x2-inch piece of white flannel
Thread, string, or ribbon for a hanger

Hollow out a place in the middle of the foam ball. If so desired, paint the ball silver or gold. Starting with a small section, smooth a thin layer of glue onto a pin, then one of the smallest beads, followed by the larger bead and a sequin. Stick the pin into the ball. Place beaded pins all around the ball, except for in the hollowed area. At the top, choose a place to anchor your hanger with a pin. In the area not covered by pins, spread a thin amount of glue, then sprinkle a generous amount of glitter to cover it. (Do this over a pan to catch the extra glitter.) Fold the flannel around the baby and secure with glue. Then glue the baby into the hollow of your ball. You can make a tiny bow to place at the top of the hollowed area.

CHARMING BALL ORNAMENTS

Buy several clear glass ball ornaments. Each one can be made to look unique and special. Remove the metal hanger from the neck of the ball to reveal an opening. Decorate the inside, then replace the hanger.

Beach Ball: Fill the ornament with tiny seashells and coral. Add a bit of sand.

Flower Ball: Take apart some colorful silk flowers and stuff them down the neck of the ornament. Cut a hole in a small doily and slip over the neck on the outside. Replace the hanger and tie a ribbon around it.

Marbled Paint Ball: Place a drop or two of paint inside the ornament and swirl it around to coat the inside, or try using a straw inserted into the neck of the ornament to blow the paint around. Use more than one color, either at the same time or with time in between for each color to dry. Paint should be thick enough to stick to the glass, but not so thick that it globs.

Nature Ball: Fill $1/3$ of the ball with birdseed. Replace the hanger. Glue a little bit of artificial pine, a cinnamon stick branch, and a tiny mushroom bird to the neck of the ball.

Photo Ball: Cut a picture into a circle to fit the clear ball. Place the front inside against the glass. Stuff colored tinsel behind the picture to hold it in place.

Popcorn Ball: Place 15–25 kernels of microwave

popcorn (wiped clean of excess oils) inside the ball. Place the ornament in a paper bag and put in the microwave for 1–2 minutes (no metal). Listen carefully for the last pop; you may not need to leave the ornament in for the full time. When done popping, carefully remove the hot ornament. Sprinkle some glitter inside on the popcorn. Replace the hanger and tie a pretty ribbon around the neck.

Potpourri Ball: Use small pieces of potpourri to fill the ball. Hang it on your tree next to a light to warm up the potpourri and release the scent.

Sand Art Ball: Fill with layers of different colored sand.

Winter Scene Ball: Place very tiny pinecones in the ball and add artificial snowflakes.

VICTORIAN HAND ORNAMENTS

2 7x5-inch squares unbleached muslin
1 7x5-inch square fusible fleece interlinings
Off-white thread
Pins
Iron

Sewing machine
8-inch length of narrow ecru satin ribbon
30 inches of 2-inch-wide ecru lace
Needle and thread
Hot-glue gun
Silk rosebuds or dried baby's breath
Sprays of dried evergreen

Trace your hand (with closed fingers) onto one of the unbleached muslin squares. Fuse the fleece onto the other square of muslin. Pin the two squares together, right sides together, and machine-stitch along the pattern lines, leaving the wrist end open. Clip the curves and turn right side out; press with hot iron. Machine-stitch finger lines through all three layers. Turn the cuff end under and tuck the ends of a ribbon loop inside for the hanger; machine-stitch. Cut the lace into three 10-inch lengths and with a needle and thread gather and hand-sew to the top of the cuff. Place the remaining two lengths side by side, overlapping edges by ¼ inch, and sew together, then gather to form a rosette and attach to cuff. With a hot-glue gun, fasten rosebuds, baby's breath, and evergreen to the center of the rosette.

CANDY TRAIN ENGINE

A great ornament or place favor.

Glue a roll of ring-shaped candy to the wide side of a package of gum. Glue 4 round peppermint candies to the bottom against the gum pack for wheels. Make a loop of narrow ribbon and glue the ends to the top of one end of the candy roll. Glue a caramel on top of the ribbon ends for an engineer's cab. To the other end of the candy roll, glue a chocolate kiss for a smokestack and another kiss on the same end of the package of gum for a plow front.

HANGING LUMINARIES

Gather an assortment of small glass jelly, baby food, and other jars. Make sure that they have the ridge around the top for screwing on a lid. Use a medium-gauge wire approximately 12–18 inches long. For each jar, twist one end around the jar, under the ridge. Make sure it is snug. Bend the remaining end straight up from the mouth of the jar and make a loop for a hanger. Add a ribbon tie around the jar's neck. Place a votive candle in each jar and fill the remaining space around the candle's bottom with rose hips. Hang an assortment of these luminaries from your porch railing or a variety of places where a candle can burn safely.

GRANDMA'S LITTLE CHRISTMAS STOCKINGS

1⅛ yards off-white cotton or muslin;
    matching thread
Assorted tan and off-white tatted lace and
    crochet scraps
Assorted off-white buttons
Assorted tan buttons
Assorted tiny brown shells

Create a simple stocking pattern approximately 3 inches wide x 12 inches long and cut out 14 stocking shapes. Sew stocking fronts to stocking backs with right sides facing. (All seam allowances are ¼ inch.) Leave top edges open. Turn under ¾ inch and slipstitch. Cut scraps of tatted lace 4 inches long to use as hangers for each of the 7 stockings. Tack to top edge of heel seams. Clip stocking curves and turn right side out. Decorate with lace, buttons, crochet scraps, and shells. May also be spruced up with holly or mistletoe.

POPCORN WREATH

Cover a straw wreath with popcorn using hot glue. An average wreath will use two bags of microwave popcorn. Once the wreath is covered with the popcorn, spray-paint with gold or use a sponge to spot dab some gold highlights to the popcorn. Add a bow, some small greenery sprigs, and other frills to the top of the wreath.

YO-YO WREATH

Cut 8 circles (3¼ inches diameter) from green Christmas fabric. Cut 8 circles (1½ inches diameter) from poster board. Leaving the thread unknotted with a long tail hanging out, make short running stitches around the circle of fabric folding ³⁄₁₆ inch of the edge under as you go. Set your poster-board circle in the center on the wrong side of the fabric, then pull the thread ends to gather the fabric circle. Tie the thread securely and trim the ends. Adjust the yo-yo so the hole is in the center. Glue a red or white button to the center hole of each yo-yo. Glue the yo-yos together by slightly overlapping the edges. Use a plastic lid or other circle as a guide as you shape the yo-yos into a circle. Glue a red bow to the top or bottom of the wreath. Make one stitch of thread through the back fabric of one yo-yo, and tie the ends in a loop for a hanger.

RIBBON TREE

5-inch Styrofoam ball
12-inch wooden dowel or squared wood
  trim, for stem
Ready-to-mix cement
Basket
Masking tape
Selection of ribbons in different colors and
  widths, about 6½ yards of each
Florist's spool wire
Reindeer moss

Spear the Styrofoam ball on the dowel. Mix enough cement to almost fill the lined basket and pour in. Place dowel in center of basket and secure with a web of masking tape across the top of pot. Let dry for 24 hours. Cut ribbon in strips 7 inches long. Double up ribbon to form single-loop bows and twist wire around center, leaving 1 long end to stud ball completely with bows. Spread reindeer moss out over base of tree.

Holiday Potpourri

4 oranges
4 lemons
½ cup whole allspice
10 cinnamon sticks, broken
½ cup whole cloves
10 bay leaves, crumbled

Use a vegetable peeler to peel fruit carefully. Remove only the peel and not the white pith. Cut or tear peel into 1-inch pieces. Spread peel on a pan lined with a paper towel. Place in oven at 175° or on the oven's warm setting. Dry for 1½ hours, turning occasionally. Peels should be leathery and slightly brittle. Let stand and air dry on a paper towel for 24 hours. Combine with remaining ingredients. Keep in airtight container. To use: Let stand in a room in an open container or put 1 tablespoon of potpourri into 2 cups of hot water.

DRIED FRUIT

Apples—Slice $1/8$–$1/4$-inch thick, including the core. Soak in lemon juice with salt for several minutes, then pat dry. They can also be sprinkled with a fruit preserver. You may want to sprinkle them with cinnamon for fragrance. Place on a lightly greased cookie sheet. Bake in a 150° oven for 6 hours. Slices should have a leathery texture. Spray with a few coats of clear acrylic.

Oranges or Lemons—On a whole orange, use a knife or citrus peeler to cut approximately 6 lines down the sides and through the peel at intervals. Place on a cookie sheet and bake in a 150° oven for 10–12 hours. For slices, cut $1/8$–$1/4$-inch thick. Place on a lightly sprayed cookie sheet. Bake in a 150° oven for 6 hours or until edges start to curl and are pliable. Spray with a few coats of clear acrylic. Use dried fruit on wreaths and garland, to enhance plain potpourri, or as an accent on almost anything like a gift, a picture frame, a tree ornament, and so on.

Additional idea: Peel lemons and oranges, making sure to keep large sections of peel. Cut shapes in the peel with tiny cookie cutters. Allow them to air dry and add to your potpourri.

FROM THE KITCHEN

"Give, and it will be given to you.
A good measure, pressed down,
shaken together and running over,
will be poured into your lap."

LUKE 6:38

Heavenly Mints

1 (16-ounce) package powdered sugar
½ cup margarine, softened
2 tablespoons evaporated milk
4 to 5 drops of peppermint flavoring
2 to 3 drops of food coloring
Rubber candy molds

Mix ingredients in a large bowl at high speed until well blended. Knead mixture until smooth. Spread paper towels over cookie sheets. Shape mixture in rubber candy molds and place shapes on cookie sheets; cover with paper towels. Mints should stand overnight and then be stored in covered containers with waxed paper between layers. Wrap each mint in plastic wrap. Then create your own angel pattern and draw angels on stiff, colored paper; cut out. Punch 2 holes in the center of each angel and pull a thin ribbon through each hole. Tie ribbon around a wrapped mint to attach it to the angel.

Chocolate-Dipped Spoons

Chocolate chips (2 ounces will do about 8 spoons)
Plastic spoons (find festive colors)

Optional flavoring extracts (almond, peppermint, anise, etc.)

Melt chips over low heat until smooth. Dip spoons
up to the start of the handle, allowing a good bit of
chocolate to pool in the bowl. You can sprinkle with
crushed candy canes while wet, or let the spoons
dry on waxed paper and drizzle white chocolate
over the dark chocolate. Try dipping half of the
spoon in white chocolate and half in dark. Wrap
dried spoons in plastic wrap and secure with ribbon.
Use as stirrers in hot coffee, cappuccino, and cocoa.

CHOCOLATE-DIPPED COOKIES

1 package white or chocolate almond bark
1 package sandwich cookies like Oreos or Nutter
   Butters (even homemade sugar cookies or
   chocolate chip cookies will work)
Edible sprinkle decorations (optional)

Melt almond bark in microwave or over low
heat. When smooth and hot, carefully dip cookies, one at a time, into almond bark, covering ½
to ¾ of cookie. Place on waxed paper and shake
on sprinkles.

CHOCOLATE-DIPPED CANDY CANES

½ cup semisweet chocolate chips or white
   vanilla chips
2 teaspoons shortening
16 peppermint candy canes or sticks
Crushed, hard peppermint candy, red and
   green
Sprinkles or miniature chocolate chips
   (optional)

Cover a cookie sheet with waxed paper. Melt
chips and shortening in a saucepan over low heat
until smooth. Dip ¾ of the candy cane in the
chocolate. Lay on the waxed paper and allow it to
cool about 2 minutes. Roll the chocolate-covered
ends in decorative peppermint, sprinkles, or chips.
Can be stored under loose cover for up to 2 weeks.

CANDIED TEA STIRRERS

30–35 pieces of fruit-flavored hard candy,
   crushed
2 tablespoons light corn syrup
Sturdy plastic spoons

Line a cookie sheet with waxed paper and spray with cooking spray. Crush candies in a heavy plastic bag with a hammer or rolling pin. Add crushed candies to corn syrup and melt over low heat in a small saucepan. Stir often. Spoon candy into bowl of each plastic spoon. Place spoons on cookie sheet, allowing handles to rest on the raised sides so that the spoons are level. Let candy harden completely before storing in an airtight container or wrapping with plastic wrap. Use the spoons to stir and add flavor to plain hot tea.

HARDTACK CANDY

1 cup water
½ cup light corn syrup
2 cups sugar
½ teaspoon flavoring for candy making
   (orange or peppermint extract, cinnamon oil, or other)
Food coloring
Powdered sugar

In a large, heavy saucepan, combine water, syrup, and sugar. Over medium heat, stir constantly until all is dissolved. Stop stirring and bring to 300° to 310°F (149° to 154°C) on a candy thermometer—or until a small amount of syrup dropped into cold water forms hard, brittle threads. Remove from heat and add flavoring and food coloring. Pour into a greased jelly roll pan and dust with powdered sugar. When cool, break into pieces. Store in airtight jars or bags.

Caramel Corn in a Gift Bag

1 cup butter or margarine
2 cups brown sugar
½ cup light corn syrup
1 teaspoon salt
½ teaspoon baking soda
1 teaspoon vanilla
5 quarts popped corn

Preheat oven to 250 degrees. In a large saucepan, melt butter over low heat. Add brown sugar, corn syrup, salt, and stir. Turn heat to high and bring to a boil for 5 minutes, stirring constantly. Remove from heat and stir in soda and vanilla. Distribute popcorn evenly between three 13x9-inch pans. Pour cooked mixture over popped corn and stir. Bake for 1 hour, removing from oven every 15 minutes to stir, to ensure even coating. Pour caramel corn onto countertop that has been covered with waxed paper and cool. Break into pieces. Give caramel popcorn in small, personally designed boxes to which colorful drawings, cutouts, and pieces of Christmas wrapping have been glued. Line box with colored tissue paper and fill with caramel corn.

CRYSTALLIZED ORANGE PECANS

1 cup sugar
$1/4$ cup orange juice
$1/4$ teaspoon ground cinnamon
2–3 cups pecan halves

Combine all of the ingredients in a $2^1/2$-quart microwave-safe bowl. Cook uncovered on 70 percent power for 6 minutes (or medium power for 7–8 minutes). Stir, then resume cooking on 70 percent power for 8–10 minutes, or until crystallized, stirring several times. Spread nuts on waxed paper, avoid having them touch, and cool. Makes 2 to 3 cups.

SPICED NUTS

2 cups whole almonds
1 teaspoon allspice
2 cups blanched peanuts
1 teaspoon cinnamon
2 cups sugar
1 teaspoon ginger
1/2 cup butter or margarine
1 teaspoon salt
3 teaspoons pumpkin pie spice

Combine all ingredients in an electric skillet. Cook approximately 15 minutes over medium heat or at 350°, stirring and coating the nuts constantly until the sugar is melted and golden brown. Spread nuts in a thin layer onto a waxed-paper or foil-lined cookie sheet to cool. Break into clusters.

MOCHA WALNUTS

1/2 cup granulated sugar
1/2 teaspoon ground cinnamon
1/2 cup brown sugar, firmly packed

¼ teaspoon ground nutmeg
½ cup sour cream
1 tablespoon instant coffee
1 teaspoon vanilla
3 cups walnut halves

In a large saucepan, combine first 6 items, mixing well. Cook over medium heat, stirring constantly, to soft ball stage (238°). Remove from heat and stir in vanilla. Add nuts, stirring to coat. Spread onto a buttered baking sheet. Cool and break into pieces. Store in airtight container.

BUTTER BLENDS

1 cup (2 sticks) of butter or margarine,
softened

Beat with one of the following groups of ingredients:

Herb: ¼–½ cup chopped fresh or 1–2 tablespoons dried herb (basil, chives, oregano, savory, tarragon, or thyme), 1 tablespoon lemon juice, and ¼ teaspoon salt

Garlic: 2 teaspoons paprika, ½ teaspoon pepper, and 8 cloves crushed garlic

Almond: 2 tablespoons finely chopped almonds and 1 teaspoon almond extract

Raspberry: 1 cup crushed raspberries and 2 tablespoons sugar or ½ cup raspberry jam

Orange: 2 teaspoons grated orange peel and 2 tablespoons orange juice

Refrigerate in tightly covered container up to 3 weeks or freeze up to 2 months. Delicious with breads, even with vegetables and meats.

Homemade Herb Vinegar

2 cups white wine vinegar
½ cup firmly packed fresh herb (basil, chives, dill weed, mint, oregano, rosemary, or tarragon)

Shake vinegar and the herb of your choice in a sealed glass jar. Allow to stand in a cool, dry place for 10 days. Strain the vinegar. Place 1 sprig of fresh herb of the same variety in a decorative jar or bottle and add strained vinegar.

Can substitute these for the herb: 6 cloves of garlic or ½ cup chopped, peeled gingerroot.

HOMEMADE FRUIT VINEGAR

3 cups white wine vinegar
2 cups of crushed berry like raspberry, blueberry, or cranberry (frozen or fresh), or ¼ cup lemon or orange rind, shredded
2 tablespoons honey

Combine in large saucepan and cover. Bring to a boil, then remove from heat and let stand until cooled. Strain the fruit or rind out. Pour into bottle(s) and seal tightly. Allow to stand at least 24 hours before adding some decorative fruit or rind to the vinegar. Seal tightly. Store at room temperature. Good for approximately 3 months.

Vinegars can be used on salads and vegetables or as marinade for meat, poultry, or fish. The bottles are pretty given unwrapped; just add a touch of ribbon or raffia to the neck.

Homemade Oil

1 cup walnuts, almonds, or hazelnuts
2 cups vegetable oil

Combine nuts and ½ cup oil in blender until nuts are finely chopped. Put nut mixture and remaining oil in a glass container. Cover tightly and allow to stand in a cool, dry place for 10 days. Strain the oil. Store in the refrigerator in a sealed glass bottle. Lasts up to 3 months. Use to accent salads and meats.

Jar Cakes

Bake a cake in a sterilized, 12-ounce, wide-mouthed canning jar. Any quick bread recipe will work, and one recipe stretches over approximately 6 jars. The cake should not bake and rise to more than ¼ to ½ inch from the jar lip. Wipe any drips from the sides. Bake one jar alone first, and gauge how much batter is right. Also gauge appropriate baking time as it can vary as much as 25 to 40 minutes. Record the figures on your recipe for the future. If you have multiple jars in the oven, move the jars during the baking process to encourage even baking. Use heavy mitts to handle the hot jars. Cover with new, boil-prepared lid and ring seal while cake is still hot. The heat should seal them. May store in a cool, dark place up to 3 months. The bread is safe to use as long as the vacuum seal holds and no mold growth appears. The jar cakes serve 1–2 people and remain very moist.

BROWNIE JAR CAKE

2 sterilized 12-ounce canning jars
1 cup flour
1 cup sugar
½ teaspoon baking soda
¼ teaspoon cinnamon
⅓ cup butter or margarine
¼ cup water
3 tablespoons cocoa
¼ cup buttermilk
1 egg, beaten
½ teaspoon vanilla
¼ cup walnuts, finely chopped (optional)

Brush melted shortening on the inside walls of sterilized jars. (Do not spray with oil or use butter.) In a small bowl, blend flour, sugar, baking soda, and cinnamon. Set aside. In a medium saucepan, combine butter, water, and cocoa. Heat over low and stir until butter melts and mixture is well blended. Remove from heat and stir in the dry mixture. Add buttermilk, egg, and vanilla. Beat by hand until smooth. Fold in nuts. Pour equally into prepared jars. Place jars on a cookie sheet in 325° oven for 35–40 minutes or until a pick inserted deep into the cake comes out clean. Remove from the oven and immediately place a hot lid onto the jars and hold snug with a ring.

GINGERBREAD JAR CAKE

5 sterilized 12-ounce canning jars
2 teaspoons ginger
2¼ cups flour
1 teaspoon cinnamon
¾ cup sugar
½ teaspoon ground cloves
1 teaspoon baking soda
½ teaspoon baking powder
¼ teaspoon salt
¾ cup margarine, softened
¾ cup water
½ cup molasses

Brush melted shortening on the inside walls of sterilized jars. (Do not spray with oil or use butter.) In a large bowl, combine dry ingredients. Stir in margarine, water, and molasses. Divide batter equally among the 5 jars (they should be about half full). Place jars on a cookie sheet in 325° oven for 35–40 minutes or until a pick inserted deep into the cake comes out clean. Remove from the oven and immediately place a hot lid onto the jars and hold snug with a ring.

Pumpkin Spice Jar Cake

8 sterilized 12-ounce canning jars
1 cup raisins, coarsely chopped
1 cup walnuts, coarsely chopped
2 teaspoons ground cloves
2 teaspoons cinnamon
1 teaspoon ginger
2 cups flour
2 teaspoons baking soda
¼ teaspoon baking powder
½ teaspoon salt
4 large eggs
2 cups sugar
1 cup oil
16 ounces pumpkin (not pie filling)

Sterilize jars and, when cooled, brush melted shortening on the inside walls. (Do not spray with oil or use butter.) Combine raisins and walnuts; set aside. Sift dry ingredients together in a large bowl. Add raisins and walnuts; set aside. In another large bowl, beat eggs at high speed 2–3 minutes until thick and yellow. Gradually beat in sugar until thick and light in color. At low speed, beat in oil and pumpkin until well blended. Divide batter among the 8 jars (should be slightly less than half full). Place jars on a cookie sheet in 325° oven for 35–40 minutes or until a pick inserted deep into the cake comes out clean. Remove from the oven and immediately place a hot lid onto the jars and hold snug with a ring.

FROZEN COOKIE DOUGH

This year give those short on time (or skill) a gift of cookie dough to bake on those cold, lazy winter evenings after the holiday goodies are gone. Plan to give each person a variety of dough. Use basic recipes for chocolate chip, oatmeal, and peanut butter cookies. Mix up double batches. Put straight into freezer-safe plastic containers or bags. Or, so only what is needed can be baked instead of the whole batch, form the dough into balls and freeze on a cookie sheet. When frozen, put them into bags and store in the freezer. Dough will last longer in the freezer than baked cookies, and the recipient will be able to enjoy the cookies warm from the oven. When you give the dough, include a note with baking instructions.

FRIENDSHIP SOUP MIX IN A JAR

½-pint or 1-quart jar
½ cup dry split peas
¼ cup dried minced onion
⅓ cup beef bouillon (low sodium)
2 teaspoons Italian seasoning
½ cup uncooked long grain brown rice
¼ cup pearl barley
½ cup dry lentils
½ cup alphabet macaroni

In a ½-pint or 1-quart jar, layer the eight ingredients in the order listed. Seal tightly. (If ingredients do not come right up to the top of the jar, you can place a crumpled piece of plastic wrap on top of the last layer to keep layers from shifting.) Store in a cool, dry place until ready to use.

Instruction card:

To prepare soup, you'll need 1 pound of lean ground beef and a 28-ounce can of diced tomatoes. Remove macaroni from top of jar and set aside. In a large saucepan or Dutch oven, brown beef and drain. Add 3 quarts of water, tomatoes with juice, and soup mix, then bring to a boil. Reduce heat and cover. Simmer for 45 minutes. Add the reserved macaroni and cover. Simmer for 15–20 minutes or until macaroni, peas, lentils, and barley are tender. Yield: 1 batch serves 16.

MEXICAN DIP MIX IN A JAR

½ cup dried parsley
⅓ cup chili powder
⅓ cup dried minced onion
¼ cup ground cumin
¼ cup dried chives
¼ cup salt

In a large bowl, combine the spices and store in an airtight container.

This dip mix can be given in a small sombrero.

Instruction card:
  3 tablespoons dip mix
  1 cup sour cream or low-fat plain yogurt
  1 cup mayonnaise (may use low-fat)

In a medium mixing bowl, combine ingredients. Whisk the mixture until smooth. Refrigerate for 2 to 4 hours. Serve with tortilla chips or fresh vegetables. Makes 2 cups.

COBBLER MIX IN A JAR

  1 cup all-purpose flour
  1 cup sugar
  1 teaspoon baking powder
  1 teaspoon powdered vanilla

Combine and blend the ingredients in a small bowl. Store in an airtight container.

Instruction card:
Serves 8 to 10
  4 cups fresh or frozen berries (blueberries, raspberries, or blackberries)
  ¼ cup orange juice
  ¼ cup sugar

1 teaspoon cinnamon
1 cup butter, melted
1 egg
1 jar cobbler mix

Preheat oven to 375°. In large mixing bowl, combine berries, juice, sugar, and cinnamon. Place berries in a 9x13-inch pan. In small mixing bowl, blend the butter with the egg. Add the cobbler mix and stir until the mixture sticks together. Drop the dough by tablespoonfuls on top of the berry filling. Bake for 35–45 minutes or until the topping is golden brown and the filling is bubbling. Allow to cool for 15 minutes before serving.

FUDGE BROWNIE MIX IN A JAR

2 cups sugar
1 cup all-purpose flour
1 cup cocoa (not Dutch process)
1 cup chopped pecans
1 cup chocolate chips

Mix all the ingredients together and store in an airtight container.

Instruction card:
Makes 24
1 cup butter or margarine, softened
4 eggs
1 jar fudge brownie mix

Preheat the oven to 325°. Grease a 9x13-inch pan. In a large bowl, cream the butter with a mixer. Add the eggs, one at a time, beating well. Add the brownie mix and continue to beat the mixture until it is smooth. Spread into the greased pan and bake for 40–50 minutes.

BLONDE BROWNIE MIX IN A JAR

16 ounces brown sugar
½ cup chopped pecans
2 cups all-purpose flour

Combine ingredients. Store in a jar or heavy plastic bag.

Instruction card:
Combine mix with 4 eggs and blend well. Pour into a greased 9x13-inch pan. Bake at 350° for 25–28 minutes.

CANDY COOKIE MIX IN A JAR

½ cup sugar
1 teaspoon powdered vanilla
½ cup brown sugar, firmly packed
1 teaspoon baking soda
2 cups flour

Combine all ingredients in a medium bowl. Whisk the ingredients together until they are evenly distributed, making sure all brown sugar lumps are crushed. Store in an airtight jar.

Instruction card:
Makes 3 dozen cookies
    1 cup unsalted butter or margarine, softened
    1 large egg
    1 jar candy cookie mix
    1 cup candy bar chunks (Reese's peanut
        butter cups, Butterfinger bars, white or
        milk chocolate chunks)

Preheat oven to 350°. In a large bowl, beat the butter with a mixer until it is smooth. Add the egg, and continue beating until the egg is well blended. Add the cookie mix and candy bar chunks and blend on low. Form the cookies into 1½-inch balls and place them 2 inches apart on an ungreased cookie sheet. Bake for 10–12 minutes, until golden on the edges. Remove from oven and cool on cookie sheet for 2 minutes.

MAGIC COOKIE BAR MIX IN A JAR

$1/4$ cup walnuts, chopped
$1/2$ cup shredded coconut
1 cup butterscotch chips
1 cup graham crackers, crushed
1 cup semisweet chocolate chips

Combine ingredients in a widemouthed glass canning jar by order listed above.

Instruction card:
Preheat oven to 350°. Add $1/2$ cup melted butter to graham crackers. Place in a 9x9-inch baking pan and pat to evenly cover the bottom. Scatter remaining ingredients on top. Pour a 14-ounce can of sweetened condensed milk evenly over everything. Bake for 30 minutes.

DOG BISCUIT MIX IN A JAR

1 cup all-purpose unbleached flour
½ cup instant nonfat dry milk powder
1 cup whole wheat flour
1 teaspoon brown sugar or white sugar
½ cup yellow cornmeal
½ teaspoon garlic powder
Pinch of salt

In a medium mixing bowl, combine all ingredients. Pour into a 1-quart, widemouthed canning jar. Close jar tightly. Tie a dog-biscuit cookie cutter and instruction card around the top of the jar with a pretty ribbon.

Instruction Card:
Position a rack in the center of the oven. Preheat to 250°. Place contents of the jar in a medium-sized bowl. Add 1 large egg, ½ cup shredded sharp cheddar cheese, ¼ cup grated Parmesan cheese, ¼ to ½ cup hot chicken broth, beef broth, or very hot water.

Make very heavy, but not sticky, dough. Add more flour or water, a spoonful at a time if dough is too moist (use flour) or too dry (use hot water).

Turn out dough onto a floured pastry cloth and knead 8–10 times until elastic. Let dough rest for 5 minutes. Roll out dough ½-inch thick and cut with a dog-bone-shaped cutter. Place cookies close together. They will not spread.

Bake for 1 hour, rotate the baking trays in the oven (turn tray around 180 degrees), and bake them another ½ hour. Cool the cookies in the pan for 1 minute, then transfer to a wire cake rack to cool completely.

GIFT BUNDLES

Each man should give what he has decided in
his heart to give,
not reluctantly or under compulsion,
for God loves a cheerful giver.

2 CORINTHIANS 9:7

Fill an inexpensive basket or other container with a variety of items that will be meaningful to a special person.

For Tea Time: A teacup. A teapot. Strainer. A variety of teas. A small jar of honey. Homemade jams or jellies with crackers or a small loaf of homemade bread. Shortbread cookies. Tea stirrers.

For Bath Time: Bath salts. Scented soaps and lotions. Sponge. Scented candle. Washcloths. Chocolate truffles. A doorknob sign that says "Pampering. Do Not Disturb."

For Family Night: A family-friendly movie on VHS or DVD or a gift certificate to a video rental store. Two bags of microwave popcorn. Theater-sized boxes of candy. Kool-Aid mix in envelopes or 4 cans of soda pop.

For the Gardener: Small hand tools (spade, trowel, rake, and cutters). Gloves. Knee pads. Plant markers. Seed packets. Bulbs. Bonemeal or other multipurpose fertilizer. (Place things in a bucket or watering can.)

For the Birdwatcher: Bird feeder. A bag of seed.

Suet with cage. Bird guidebook. Rain gauge. Outdoor thermometer.

For the Do-It-Yourself Person: Tape measure. Hammer. Screwdriver with changeable heads. Variety box of nails and screws. Small level. Tool apron. Utility knife. Safety glasses. Superglue. Duct tape. How-to book.

For the Writer: Stationery. Pens. Envelopes. Stamps. Postcards. Address book (with some special addresses already included).

For the Teacher: Colorful pencils. Erasers. Post-it notepads. Packets of stickers. Red pens. Highlighters.

For the Student: Calculator. Notebooks. Pencils, pens, and highlighters. Study lamp. Dictionary and thesaurus. Post-it notepads in various sizes.

For the New Mom: A large bottle of pain reliever. Hand lotion. A picture frame. A brag book. A CD of favorite lullabies. Chocolate. Coffee. Coupons promising your baby-sitting services.

For the Baby: A boo-boo bunny. First Christmas ornament. Containers of powder, baby lotion, baby wash or shampoo, diaper rash ointment, and baby wipes. Washcloths. Burping cloths. Receiving blankets. A teething ring. Pacifier. Bib. Night light. (Place in a diaper bag or small waste can.)

For the Cook: Measuring spoons and cups. Spices. Apron. Kitchen timer. Recipe box or other organizer. Cookbook. Small mixing bowls. Whisk. Box of storage bags. (Use a large mixing bowl or colander lined with a dish towel to hold things.)

For the Outdoor Chef: Barbecue tools. Aluminum foil. Lighter fluid. Apron. Citronella candles. Bug spray. (Place everything in a cooler.)

For the Book Lover: Two or three new books. Small reading lamp. Bookmark. Packets of coffee or tea. Cookies.

For the Chocolate Lover: A package of candy bars. Brownies with fudge icing. Truffles. German chocolate cake. Several variations of fudge. Chocolate syrup. A couple packages of chocolate pudding mix. Chocolate covered pretzels. Chocolate/fudge butter cookies. Hot chocolate mix.

For the Car Lover: A steering-wheel cover. An ice scraper. A sun shade. A fire extinguisher. Some silly fuzzy dice. An air freshener. A bottle of car wash, tire cleaner, spot remover, and car wax. A buffer cloth. (Use a bucket to hold everything.)

For the Sports Lover: A sports blunders video. Small game balls. A pack of trading cards. Ball cap.

For the Coffee Lover: A special coffee cup. A variety of small packets of flavored coffee. Small jar of creamer (also available in flavors). Bean grinder. Chocolate-dipped cinnamon sticks or spoons. Butter cookies.

For the Pet Lover: A ball. Squeak toys. Chews. Treats. Book on pet care. Collar, leash, and name tag. Bowl with pet's name on it.

HOLIDAY CANDLES

"The Lord Jesus himself said:
'It is more blessed to give
than to receive.'"
ACTS 20:35

COOKIE-CUTTER CANDLES

Sheets of various colored beeswax (available
  at craft stores)
Cutting board
Cookie cutters
Candlewick (available at craft stores)
Hair dryer

Place sheets of beeswax individually on cutting
board. Cut 6 shapes from beeswax using 1 cookie
cutter. Insert wick in the center of the wax layers, leaving ½ inch at the top of the candle. Press
wax shapes together. If they are not adhering
well enough, heat slightly with hair dryer. Be
sure to burn candles on a nonflammable surface
or on another piece of beeswax.

CANDLED APPLES

13 large yellow apples
13 tea lights or votive candles
Lemon juice
Boxwood leaves
Lemons or limes
Thick toothpicks
Footed cake plate

To stabilize apples, cut slices from bottoms. Place a tea light on top of each apple and, with a knife, trace around candle. Cut down and scoop out enough of apple to allow all of candle to rest below the rim. Sprinkle lemon juice on apple to prevent browning. Cover a cake plate with box-wood leaves and place 5 apples in an evenly spaced circle. Place lemons or limes in center of circle. Stick toothpicks into bottom of 4 of the remaining apples and place on top of lemons, securing with toothpicks. Repeat with 3 more apples and then with last 1 to create a pyramid.

Frosted Pinecone Candleholders

12 medium-sized, upright pinecones
16-ounce box of paraffin wax
Wire cutters
Large, empty coffee can
2 packages of red wax dye
Metal tongs
Waxed paper
12 3–4-inch-long red candles
Heavy saucepan
Metal spoon

Place pinecones in freezer for 3 hours. Heat water in saucepan over low heat. Place box of paraffin wax in coffee can and set can in saucepan; when wax is completely melted, add wax dye and mix with spoon. Keep heat just warm enough to maintain liquid state. Remove pinecones from freezer and clip out top center of each with wire cutters. Dip pinecones in melted paraffin with tongs, 1 at a time. Drain on waxed paper. Holding candle by the wick, dip ½ inch of base into paraffin and stand candle in center of pinecone, pressing downward until candle is securely stuck to pinecone. Drip extra wax around the base of each candle. Cool completely.

HOLIDAY KITCHEN CANDLE

Metal kitchen grater
Artificial or real holly or any other winter
  greenery
Hot-glue gun and hot-glue sticks
Ribbon
Candle

Wash grater well and dry. Arrange greenery as

desired and glue together. Glue piece to kitchen tool; tie a bow around handle of grater and place candle inside.

Christmas Teacup Candles

Small china teacups
Candle wax
Empty coffee can
Coloring for wax or old candles
White birthday candles
White glitter

Warm teacups with hot water while wax is melting in coffee can that has been placed in a pan of water on stove. Color wax with candle coloring or old candles; remove from heat. Empty cups and dry thoroughly. Pour wax carefully into cups and allow to set for 2 or 3 minutes or until a soft covering appears on top of wax. Push a birthday candle into the wax and hold until it stands up straight. Add glitter to surface of wax.

CRAFTY GIFTS

Share with God's people. . . .
Practice hospitality.
ROMANS 12:13

LACEY BOTTLES

Lace motifs and trims as desired to fit bottles
(available at craft and fabric stores)
Assorted bottles or small flower vases
Mod Podge decoupage medium (available
from any craft store)
Small paintbrush

Experiment with placement of lace on the bottle until you are pleased with the arrangement. In order to fit the curvature of the bottle, trim some of the connecting threads so the points can be spread out. Spread Mod Podge on the bottle with a paintbrush in the basic shape of the trim. Place the lace over the brushed area and cover thoroughly with Mod Podge; let dry.

FAMILY TREE

18-inch-long paper-covered wire—
example, 36 pieces for 18 family members
Glue
Ribbon
1½-inch photo of each family member

Dried flowers
6x6-inch piece of 1½-inch-thick green
  Styrofoam
Sheet moss
Boxwood leaves

Begin by twisting together all of the pieces of covered wire about 2 inches from the bottom and continue upwards about 6 inches. Fan the bottom pieces out to form the "roots" of the tree. At the top of the twist, begin to divide the "branches" into groups of 4, fanning them out on both sides of the tree. Separate the strands of each group of 4 and fan out also. Trim ends of branches with scissors when finished to achieve realistic tree shape. Glue a two-inch ribbon loop to each photo. Then glue around perimeter of each photo and sprinkle with dried flowers to create frame effect. Cover Styrofoam with sheet moss and stick roots of tree in Styrofoam. Glue boxwood leaves to tree branches to simulate an evergreen tree and hang photos of family members to tree in generational order.

Vacation Memory Box

Old wooden or cardboard box with an
attached lid
Glue
Vacation souvenirs: postcards, ticket stubs,
small amounts of money (if foreign), street
maps, photos, seashells

Leave box standing open and glue small items
such as money, stamps, or seashells around the
edges of the box and lid. Arrange items of your
choice decoratively throughout interior of box.

Ribbon Pillow

2 13-inch squares of solid color fabric
Board
Pushpins
Assortment of ribbons, each 13 inches long
Cording
Stuffing for 12-inch pillow

Attach square of fabric to board with pushpins.
At upper left corner of fabric, place one ribbon
going horizontally and another vertically. Using

traditional basket weave, add ribbons along the top and side, weaving in and out until square is completed. Pin ribbons to the fabric and then remove from board. Sew ribbons down and attach second piece of fabric as backing. Sew on color-coordinated cording all the way around, leaving an opening. Add pillow and stitch closed.

SURPRISE ROLLS

Cardboard tubing from wrapping paper,
   paper towels, waxed paper, aluminum foil,
   or toilet tissue
Brightly colored crepe paper
Long piece of ribbon for curling
Assorted candies, treats, and snacks
Glue
Glitter
Christmas stickers

Cut tubes into equal length sections (about 3½ inches long). Place the cardboard tube on paper and roll up, pinching paper together at one end and tying with a piece of curling ribbon. Fill tube with treats, pinch other end, and tie with more curling ribbon. Open twisted ends, and decorate with glue and glitter or Christmas stickers.

ALMOND BUNCHES

2 4-inch squares of net (green and red, or 2 other
   contrasting colors)
3 sugared almonds
¼-inch-wide gold ribbon, 18 inches long

With 2 net squares, 1 on top of the other, place almonds in center of net and bring up corners to make a bag. Fold the ribbon in half and make a single stitch about 4 inches from the fold. Hold the ribbon loop behind the almond bunch and tie loose ends at the front in a bow.

GIFT WRAP, CARDS, NOTES, AND TAGS

Every good and perfect gift is from above,
coming down from the Father
of the heavenly lights,
who does not change like shifting shadows.
JAMES 1:17

DESIGN YOUR OWN GIFT WRAP!

Be creative by combining and designing with the following:

Brown packing paper or white butcher paper
  or even large brown paper grocery bags
Paint
Design tools (sponge, cotton balls, tooth-
  brush, old pot scrubber, straw to blow paint)
Rubber stamps and ink
Stickers

FAMILY PHOTO WRAPS

Family photographs
White mat board in size desired
Clear tape

Arrange photographs on white mat board, over-lapping as desired. Secure backs of photographs to mat board with small rings of tape. Photo-copy arrangement at a copy center in black and white to make your wrapping paper. Size can be reduced to use wrapping for smaller gifts.

Reusable Wraps

As an alternative to store-bought paper that can get expensive, try wrapping a box in something that can be reused by the recipient.

Bandana or scarf
Pillowcase
Blanket
Tablecloth
Fabric
Towel
Laundry bag
Tulle, netting, or lace

Window Bag

Cut a design out on one side of a sturdy bag. Cover the cutout on the inside with clear or colored plastic wrap. Fill the bag, then fold the top over, letting a hint of the contents show through. With a hole punch, put two holes at least 1 inch apart in the top fold. Put ribbon, raffia, or yarn through the holes and tie a bow that hangs above the window.

FABRIC GIFT BAGS

Cut a 16x19-inch rectangle of holiday fabric for each bag. Lay a 2-foot piece of narrow cord or ribbon along the 19-inch side and turn 1 inch of fabric over the cord, wrong sides facing. Stitch ¼ inch from the edge. Fold the 16-inch sides together with right sides facing. Stitch a ½-inch seam around the 3 rough sides. Trim the corners, and turn right side out.

Shortcut:
Cut 2 pieces of calico, flannel, or felt with pinking shears to 9x12 inches. With wrong sides facing, sew ½-inch seam. (You could hand-sew it with embroidery floss.) Fill the bag with a small gift, gather the top closed, and secure with a ribbon or raffia bow.

FABRIC ENVELOPES

To make a fabric envelope that will measure 5x8 inches, cut a piece of holiday fabric 8x13 inches with pinking shears. Measure 3 inches up the long side and mark it with a pin (you'll have a 3-inch flap). Fold the 8-inch end up to the pin (wrong sides facing) so that your pouch area will be 5 inches deep. Sew a ½-inch seam around the 3 sides of the pouch area. Cut a small slit in the center of the flap, ¾-inch from the unsewn edge of the flap. Lay the flap over the pouch and mark where the slit touches the pouch. Fold a 6–8-inch piece of ¼-inch ribbon in half and, at the fold, hand-sew it onto the pouch at the mark. Fill your pouch with the gift, fold flap over, and secure with ribbon.

POTATO PRINT CHRISTMAS CARDS

Thin cardboard in different colors
Potato
Felt-tip pen
Knife
Poster paints

Cut out 8x4-inch rectangles from festive colored cardboard and fold in half. Cut a potato in half and, using a felt-tip pen, draw around desired shape (star, holly, bell, tree) onto potato. Carefully cut around shape with a small kitchen knife. Dip surface of potato into a saucer of diluted poster paint and press potato firmly down on scrap paper to test. If print is sketchy, carefully slice off tip to make flatter. Print your cards!

GIFT TAGS

Print free gift tag designs from the Internet.

Print your own tag design onto a sheet of computer labels.

Simply fold a rectangular piece of matching wrapping paper in half for a little card tag.

Use a bookmark or other card with sentiment that you can write the name on.

Buy a key chain, ink pen, magnet, jewelry pin, or other item with the recipient's name preprinted on it.

ORNAMENT TAGS

Buy inexpensive, plain-colored ornaments with matte finish. Use a pointed, permanent marker to write the recipient's name.